SPIRAL

by Abigail Hood

Published by Playdead Press 2023

© Abigail Hood 2023

Abigail Hood has asserted her rights under the Copyright, Design and Patents Act, 1988, to be identified as the author of this work.

A CIP catalogue record for this book is available from the British Library.

ISBN 978-1-915533-16-6

Caution

All rights whatsoever in this play are strictly reserved and application for performance should be sought through the author before rehearsals begin. No performance may be given unless a license has been obtained.

This book is sold subject to the condition that it shall not by way of trade or otherwise, be lent, resold, hired out, or otherwise circulated without the publisher's prior consent in any form of binding or cover other than that in which it is published and without a similar condition including this condition being imposed on the subsequent purchaser.

Playdead Press
www.playdeadpress.com

The Jermyn Street Theatre production of *Spiral* opened on 2nd August 2023 with the following cast:

LEAH	**Abigail Hood**
TOM	**Jasper Jacob**
MARK	**Kevin Tomlinson**
GILL	**Rebecca Crankshaw**

CREATIVES

Director	**Kevin Tomlinson**
Stage Manager	**Lucy Napier**
Set Designer	**Felix Waters**
Marketing Photography	**Hannah Veale**
Marketing Design	**Andrew Harvey**
Production Photography	**Mark Dawson**
Sound Design	**Paul Furnival**
Videography	**Holly-Rose Tomlinson**

Spiral was first performed at the Park Theatre on 7th August 2018. The cast was as follows:

LEAH	**Abigail Hood**
TOM	**Adam Morris**
MARK	**Kevin Tomlinson**
GILL	**Tracey Wilkinson**

Directed by **Kevin Tomlinson** & **Glen Walford**

Abigail Hood | Leah

Since graduating from the Oxford School of Drama, Abigail's theatre credits have included: *Monster* (Park Theatre – OFFIE nominated for Best Leading Performance in a Play); *Private Peaceful* (Nottingham Playhouse / Jonathan Church no.1 tour); *Spiral, The Answer* (Park Theatre); *Dangling* (Southwark Playhouse); *Bleeding Hearts* (Bolton Octagon); *Romeo and Juliet* (Salisbury Playhouse); *All The Little Lights* (Derby Theatre); *Weapons of Happiness* (Finborough Theatre); *The Snow Queen* (Stephen Joseph Theatre); *The Lesson Before Break* (Theatre503); *True Love Waits* (Latitude Festival); *Whispering Happiness* (Tristan Bates); *The Bomb* (Lancaster Dukes) and the original production of *That Face* (Royal Court).

Her TV/Film credits include: *The Bill* (ITV); *The Things I See* (BBC) and *The Lesson* (Urban Fox).

Jasper Jacob | Tom

Jasper Jacob has been an actor since leaving University, where he studied music. His previous theatre credits include: *Execution of Justice, Dangling* (Southwark Playhouse); *Futurists, Pravda* (National Theatre); *A Woman of No Importance* (Haymarket); *Dial M for Murder* (Milford Haven); *How the Other Half Loves* (Southwold); *WildDuck* (Phoenix).

Film / TV includes: *My Name Is Lizzie*; *Pennyworth*; *Cursed*; *The Crown III*; *Father Brown*; *White Gold*; *Victoria II*; *Decline and Fall; Letters from Baghdad; Call the Midwife; New Tricks; The Honourable Woman; The Escape Artist; May Day; The Iron Lady; The Rite; Appropriate Adult; Land Girls; Peep Show; Hughie Green; Most Sincerely; Wallander, RocknRolla; Life Begins; Ultimate Force; The Government Inspector; Tell Me Lies; The Truth Game; Byron; Trevor's World of Sport; The Falklands Play; Ali G In Da House; Spooks; The Hunt; Four Fathers; A Certain Justice; Inspector Morse; Touching Evil; Underworld; Harry Enfield and Chums; Final Passage; Drop the Dead Donkey* and *House of Eliott*. Many years ago he was Darth Vadar's shuttle pilot in *Return of the Jedi*.

Kevin Tomlinson | Mark

Kevin trained with Philippe Gaulier, Keith Johnstone and on the BA Acting Course at Middlesex University.

Theatre credits include: *Monster, Spiral, Beneath the Blue Rinse, The Answer* (Park Theatre); *The Ragged Child* (Royal and Derngate Theatre); *Flat 73* (Cheltenham Everyman / UK tour); *Whose Story Is It Anyway?* (Theatre Royal, Bury St Edmunds); *Facing It Out* (Told by an Idiot, BAC); *Ramblin' Rose* (Royal and Derngate Theatre); *Madame Tellier's Establishment* (Trestle TC, Brighton Gardner AC); *Seven Ages* (Stephen Joseph Theatre / UK tour); *On The Edge!* (York Theatre Royal / UK tour).

Kevin has worked with the legendary Keith Johnstone (author of *Impro*) on numerous occasions, taking the lead role in several of his plays including *Damian* and *The Invitation*. Kevin also performed alongside the cast of *Whose Line is It Anyway?* at the Hackney Empire, in a fund raiser for the Royal

Court Theatre (directed by Keith Johnstone and Phellim McDermott).

Film /TV credits include: *Devil's Harvest* and *A Midsummer Night's Dream* for BBC2 (Open University).

Rebecca Crankshaw | Gill

Rebecca most recently appeared in *Dismissed* at Soho theatre. Her other theatre credits include *Everything That Rises Must Dance* (Complicité); *Prurience* (Southbank Centre); *Hookup* and *Affection* (Outbox Theatre); *Stop Kiss* (Above the Stag); *The Unholy Marriage of Slice and Sweetly* (ImmerCity); *10* (Vault Festival); *One Minute* (Barn Theatre, Cirencester); *The Open Couple* (The Albany); *The Spanish Tragedy* (Old Red Lion). She also understudied Lesley Sharp in Kae Tempest's *Paradise* at the National Theatre.

TV includes *Coronation Street* and *Doctors*. Film includes the upcoming Paramount production *Apartment 7A* and Jessica Hausner's *Club Zero*.

Rebecca was awarded a Norman Beaton Fellowship in 2021 which resulted in a six month contract with the BBC Radio Drama Company in 2022.

Abigail Hood | Writer

Abigail's previous credits include: *Monster* and *Spiral* (Park Theatre), *Dangling* (Southwark Playhouse) and *Atlantis* (Old Fire Station, Oxford).

Lucy Napier | Stage Manager

Lucy is a graduate of the Guildford School of Acting. Her credits include *Kerry Jackson* and *Connections Festival* (National Theatre); *The Rocky Horror Picture Show* (UK tour) and the first UK production of Irving Berlin's *Holiday Inn*.

Kevin Tomlinson | Director

Kevin is the artistic director of KEPOW Theatre Company, associate director of Veritas Theatre Company and a past winner of the Rose Bruford Trust Directors Award. In the summer of 2022, Kevin directed the world premiere of *Monster* at London's Park Theatre, which was nominated for three Off-West-End Awards (OFFIES).

He has directed over forty-five plays professionally, to date, including several plays for the British Council in Singapore. His passion for new writing and adapting classics, has led him to direct productions in: New Zealand, America, South Korea, Malaysia, Norway, Germany, Holland, France, UAE, and Bali.

For two years, Kevin was the writer-in-residence at the Royal and Derngate Theatre in Northampton. His play *Who?* was performed upstairs at the Royal Court Theatre in London, having won the Sunday Times Playwright Award.

Kevin has also worked with the legendary Keith Johnstone (author of *Impro*) on a number of occasions –directing several world premieres of Keith's plays in Canada; most notably the highly successful, sell-out production of *Open Season.*

VERITAS THEATRE COMPANY

Veritas is a UK based theatre company specialising in challenging and provocative new writing.

The company seeks to give a voice to new British writers who have something to say about the world we live in today. The themes and actions within these new plays may be highly amusing or highly disturbing but – either way – are always based on a desire to tell the truth as the writer sees it. Hence the name of the company; Veritas (the goddess of truth in Roman mythology).

KEPOW THEATRE COMPANY

Kepow are an Oxford based theatre company committed to creating innovative, exciting, dynamic theatre that appeals to a wide demographic. Their shows involve a combination of comedy, pathos, improvisation and mask work.

Since 2003 Kepow's shows have toured internationally to 14 countries on 4 continents, including: New Zealand, Canada, Hong Kong, Singapore, South Korea, Germany, Norway, Bali, Hawaii, UAE, France and Holland.

JERMYN STREET THEATRE

Honorary Patron
HRH Princess Michael of Kent

Patron
Sir Michael Gambon

Board of Trustees
Penny Horner
Howard Jameson (Chair)
Chris Parkinson
Vikram Sivalingam
Peter Wilson

Advisory Board
Almiro Andrade
Terri Donovan
Keith MacDonald
Leslie Macleod-Miller
Amma-Afi Osei
Paulette Randall MBE
Sarah Reuben
Geraldine Terry
Johanna Town
Jatinder Verma MBE
Peter Wilson

Artistic Director
Stella Powell-Jones

Executive Director
Penny Horner

Executive Producer
David Doyle

Carne Deputy Director
Anna Ryder*

Producer
Gabriele Uboldi

Production Manager
Lucy Mewis-McKerrow

Marketing Manager
Natasha Ketel

Graphic Designer
Ciaran Walsh

PR
David Burns

Marketing Assistant
Isobel Griffiths

Digital Advertising
Hannah Azuonye

Venue Technician
Edward Callo

Business Development
Chris Parkinson

Associate Designer
Louie Whitemore

Associate Artists
Darren Sinnott
Ebenezer Bamgboye

Box Office Manager
Alex Pearson

Box Office Supervisor
Emily Richelle

Day Staff
Laura Jury-Hyde
Grace Wessels**

Duty Managers
Christina Gazelidis
Adam Ishaq
Adam Lilley

Bar Team
Mandy Berger
Aren Johnston
Laura Jury-Hyde
Pippa Lee
Scarlett Stitt

Web Design
Robin Powell / Ideasfor

Web Development
Robert Iles / Dynamic Listing

Jermyn Street Theatre is a Registered Charity No. 11869

Creative Associates
Brigitte Adela
Douglas Baker
Safaa Benson-Effiom
Antonia Georgieva
Ben Grant
Laura Howard
Natalie Johnson
Bella Kear
Jaisal Marmion
Ada Rocci Ruiz

*The Carne Deputy Director position is supported by Philip & Christine Carne.

**Membership Manager

With thanks to Leslie Macleod-Miller for his sponsorship of the **Sandra Macleod-Miller Mini Bar**.

Jermyn Street Theatre staff salaries are supported by **Backstage Trust**

The Creative Associates programme & Footprints Festival are supported using public funding by the National Lottery through **Arts Council England** and by: **Philip Carne MBE & Christine Carne, the Noël Coward Foundation, the Maria Björnson Memorial Fund, the Harold Hyam Wingate Foundation, the Teale Charitable Trust,** and the **Unity Theatre Trust.**

a small theatre with big stories

WHO WE ARE

Jermyn Street Theatre is a unique theatre in the heart of the West End: a home to remarkable artists and plays, performed in the most intimate and welcoming of surroundings. World-class, household-name playwrights, directors and actors work here alongside people just taking their first steps in professional theatre. It is a crucible for multigenerational talent.

The programme includes outstanding new plays, rare revivals, new versions of European classics, and high-quality musicals, alongside one-off musical and literary events. We collaborate with theatres across the world, and our productions have transferred to the West End and Broadway. Recently, our pioneering online work and theatre-on-film has been enjoyed across the world.

A registered charity No. 1186940, Jermyn Street Theatre was founded in 1994 with no core funding from government or the Arts Council. Since then, the theatre has survived and thrived thanks to a mixture of earned income from box office sales and the generous support of individual patrons and trusts and foundations. In 2017, we became a producing theatre, the smallest in London's West End. Around 60% of our income comes from box office sales, and the rest in charitable support and private funding.

"Unerringly directed ...no one in this tiny theatre dared breathe."
The Observer

From top: Jack Reitman in *Thrill Me: The Leopold & Loeb Story*, 2022; Jennifer Kirby in *The Massive Tragedy of Madame Bovary*, 2022. Photos by Steve Gregson.

> "An unexpected treat of the highest order."
> *The Evening Standard*

OVER THE YEARS

1930s During the 1930s, the basement of 16b Jermyn Street was home to the glamorous Monseigneur Restaurant and Club.

Early 1990s The staff changing rooms were transformed into a theatre by Howard Jameson and Penny Horner (who continue to serve as Chair of the Board and Executive Director today) in the early 1990s and Jermyn Street Theatre staged its first

1994 production in August 1994.

1995 Neil Marcus became the first Artistic Director in 1995 and secured Lottery funding for the venue; producer Chris Grady also made a major contribution to the theatre's development.

Late 1990s In 1995, HRH Princess Michael of Kent became the theatre's Patron and David Babani, subsequently the Artistic Director of the Menier Chocolate Factory, took over as Artistic Director until 2001. Later Artistic Directors included Gene David Kirk and Anthony Biggs.

2012 The theatre won the Stage Award for Fringe Theatre of the Year.

2017 Tom Littler restructured the theatre to become a full-time producing house.

2020 Our audiences and supporters helped us survive the damaging impacts of the Covid-19 lockdown and we were able to produce a season of largely digital work, including the award-winning 15 Heroines with Digital Theatre +.

2021 We won the Stage Award for Fringe Theatre of the Year for a second time. Artistic Director Tom Littler and Executive Director Penny Horner were recognised in The Stage 100.

2022 2022 We won a Critics' Circle Award for Exceptional Theatre-Making During Lockdown and an OffWestEnd Award for our Artistic Director.

Stella Powell-Jones and David Doyle succeeded Tom Littler as Artistic Director and Executive Producer respectively, working alongside Executive Director Penny Horner to form a management team of three.

David Threlfall in *Beckett Triple Bill*, 2020. Photo by Tristram Kenton

support us

"I recently became a Patron of Jermyn Street Theatre, as I believe passionately in the work it is doing. It would be wonderful if you could contribute."

Sir Michael Gambon

Become a Friend of the theatre and enjoy a range of exclusive benefits. Join one of our four tiers of Friends with names inspired by *The Tempest* from just £50 a year.

Lifeboat Friends

(From £4.50 a month)
Our Lifeboat Friends are the heart of Jermyn Street Theatre. Their support keeps us going. Rewards include priority booking to ensure they can get the best seats in the house.

The Ariel Club

(From £12.50 a month)
Members of the Ariel Club enjoy exclusive access to the theatre and our team. As well as the priority booking and Friends Nights enjoyed by Lifeboat Friends, Ariel Club members also enjoy a range of other benefits.

The Miranda Club

(From £45 a month)
Members of the Miranda Club enjoy all the benefits of the Ariel Club, and they enjoy a closer relationship with the theatre.

The Director's Circle

(From £250 a month)
The Director's Circle is an exclusive inner circle of our biggest donors. They are invited to every press night and enjoy regular informal contact with our Artistic Director and team. They are the first to hear our plans and often act as a valuable sounding board. We are proud to call them our friends.

We only have seventy seats which makes attending our theatre a magical experience but even if we sell every seat, we still need to raise more funds.

Michael Gambon, Sinéad Cusack, Richard Griffiths, David Warner, Joely Richardson, Danny Lee Wynter, Rosalie Craig, Trevor Nunn, Adjoa Andoh, David Suchet, Tuppence Middleton, Martina Laird, Gemma Whelan, Eileen Atkins, Jimmy Akingbola and many more have starred at the theatre.

But even more importantly, hundreds of young actors and writers have started out here.

If you think you could help support our theatre, then please visit
www.jermynstreettheatre.co.uk/friends/

Jermyn Street Theatre is a Registered Charity No. 1186940. 60% of our income comes from box office sales and the remaining 40% comes from charitable donations. That means we need your help.

our friends

The Ariel Club

Richard Alexander
David Barnard
Derek Baum
Martin Bishop
Sarah Dobson
Dmitry Bosky
Katie Bradford
Nigel Britten
Christopher Brown
Donald Campbell
James Carroll
Ted Craig
Jeanette Culver
Shomit Dutta
Jill & Paul Dymock
Lucy Fleming
Anthony Gabriel
Carol Gallagher
Roger Gaynham
Paul Guinery
Debbie Guthrie
Diana Halfnight
Julie Harries
Eleanor Harvey
Andrew Hughes
Mark Jones
Margaret Karliner
David Lanch
Caroline Latham
Isabelle Laurent
Christine MacCallum
Keith Macdonald
Vivien Macmillan-Smith
Nicky Oliver
Sally Padovan
Kate & John Peck
Adrian Platt
Alexander Powell
Oliver Prenn
Martin Sanderson
Carolyn Shapiro
Nigel Silby
Philip Somervail
Robert Swift
Gary Trimby
George Warren
Lavinia Webb
Ann White
Ian Williams
John Wise

The Miranda Club

Anonymous
Anthony Ashplant
Geraldine Terry
Gyles & Michèle Brandreth
Sylvia de Bertodano
Robyn Durie
Maureen Elton
Nora Franglen
Mary Godwin
Ros & Alan Haigh
Nick Hern
Marta Kinally
Yvonne Koenig
Hilary Lemaire
Jane Mennie
Charles Paine
John & Terry Pearson
Iain Reid
Ros Shelley
Martin Shenfield
Carol Shephard-Blandy
Jenny Sheridan
Sir Bernard Silverman
Brian Smith
Frank Southern
Mark Tantam
Paul Taylor
Brian & Esme Tyers

Director's Circle

Anonymous
Judith Burnley
Philip Carne MBE &
Christine Carne
Jocelyn Abbey & Tom
Carney
Colin Clark RIP
Lynette & Robert Craig
Gary Fethke
Flora Fraser
Robert & Pirjo Gardiner
Charles Glanville & James
Hogan
Crawford & Mary Harris
Judith Johnstone
Ros & Duncan McMillan
Leslie & Peter MacLeod-Miller
James L. Simon
Marjorie Simonds-Gooding
Peter Soros & Electra Toub
Fiona Stone
Melanie Vere Nicoll
Robert Westlake & Marit Mohn

WHY I WROTE *SPIRAL*

'Dear Steven, we love you, we miss you. We hope you found what you were looking for.' A few years ago I saw this printed in the bottom corner of a free London newspaper and it caught the breath in my throat. For unlike the usual pleas for missing people to return this was something quite other. In my mind it was written by Steven's parents yet in this century there was no sense of panic or desperation but, instead, a quiet acceptance and selfless parental desire for a child to find peace no matter what the cost to themselves.

I couldn't stop thinking about the people that had sent in that entry; how long has Steven been gone? Why had they, seemingly, given up hope of him coming home? Had they given up all hope? Why did they think he had gone? Was it a shock when he left? Did they think he would see the entry in the newspaper? What did they hope it would achieve? How had they reached a place where they had accepted what he had done? My mind was reeling. If the person I loved most in the world walked out of my life, how would I feel? How would I go on? Would I ever stop searching? Would I ever be able to move on from that? Or would that event define me for the rest of my life? It was these questions that prompted me to write a play exploring how people cope in the worst imaginable situation, the strategies they may use and how they would manage to go on living when in a state of limbo, waiting and aching for someone's return.

Well, that was where it began and is where the play begins... two characters; a middle aged man and a young woman, both of whom have suffered a significant person disappearing from their lives... but, as with all things, once I started to write I found that one question led to another and another and the play is now about many things and my imaginings pushed to their most extreme.

Steven, I hope you found what you were looking for but, as much as this, I hope that the people you left behind found the peace that they found themselves searching for when you left.

Abigail Hood

DIRECTOR'S NOTE

Abigail's writing reminds me of the Greek writers Euripides and Socrates. Or the Russian playwright Anton Chekhov. Her characters are so flawed, vulnerable, and desperately in need. They behave irresponsibly, make wild choices or carry out shocking actions because they are wounded, scared, hurting or simply filled with an overpowering emotion or desire for something or someone. They are, in essence, human. And they are beautifully imperfect. That is what makes them so interesting. It's why we root for them, or hate them, try to understand them and care what happens to the them; whether it be punishment or redemption. The vast majority of Abigail's characters are essentially 'good' human beings, who find themselves in painfully complex emotional situations, without any clear solutions easily available.

Spiral is a play that features four such human beings, struggling with a huge need for love and battling a strong sense of not being in control of their lives. Life, for all of them, is painful and confusing. They are all dealing with past trauma and, in the process, several of them inflict new traumas on each other. This makes *Spiral* a challenging play to watch or read, but also incredibly gripping. One is constantly asking: would I do that? Or 'what would happen if...'? No easy answers are provided. But then, life is not easy for most people.

On the flip side, what also makes Abigail's writing a pleasure to watch, read or direct is that it also offers hope. This hope may sometimes be tinged with other darker emotions but Abigail is definitely not a writer with a nihilistic outlook or pessimistic world view. No Weltschmerz is to be detected in her writing. She is a writer who is neither simplistically optimistic nor depressingly pessimistic. She is simply authentically realistic. Perhaps this is because all of her plays, to date, have been based on meticulous research and a keen eye for observing real life? I sense this is one of the main reasons why her plays are so captivating. They are honest and they depict reality.

Whatever the dark topics, themes or events within the play, there is always humour, love and kindness to be found too. There is always the yin to balance the yang in her writing. There is always a sense of essentially good people coping the best they can in emotionally complicated situations. And there is always a sense that there is light at the end of the tunnel; no matter how faint or far away that light is.

So, with all that in mind, I hope you find watching or reading this play as intellectually and emotionally absorbing as I have found it to direct.

Kevin Tomlinson

With special thanks to:

Richard Prouse, Natasha Hancock, Renata Allen, PJ, Kara Young, Gill and Jerry Hood, Holly-Rose Tomlinson, Pollyanna Knight, Jude Thorp, Nomi Everall, Glen Walford, Maggie Saunders, Ian Gain, Charlotte Brooke, Philip D. McQuillan, Chris Lane, Jackie Deane, Tracey Wilkinson, Stephan Boyce, Paul Ansdell, Tom Glover, Steve Turnbull and Adam Morris.

For Kevin – because you believe in me

CHARACTERS (in order of appearance):

TOM *late 50's – early 60's*

LEAH *mid-late 20's*

GILL *mid-late 50's*

MARK *mid-late 30's*

A slash in the dialogue (/) indicates that the next actor should start their line, creating overlapping speech.

SCENE 1

London. A park. Tom waits. Looks at watch. Moments pass. Leah enters, she is dressed in a school uniform.

TOM: Where've you been? I said 4 o'clock by the fountain

LEAH: I had detention

TOM: Oh, very good, good. /But

LEAH: It won't happen again

TOM: Ok, it's fine, it's fine, let's just carry on

He looks at her. Beat.

>Wow, you're *(he smiles)* really quite perfect...great hair, exactly right, love the make-up – just pushing the limit. *(pause)* Perfect. *(beat)* And just the right size

Leah smiles.

LEAH: So, what do you want me to do...?

TOM: Talk for a bit?

LEAH: Sure

TOM: Then... some food perhaps? McDonalds maybe?

LEAH: Fine

TOM: Let me take your bag

LEAH: No, I usually keep it with / me during

TOM: I have to carry the bag

LEAH: Please, I'd / rather

TOM: We have to keep it accurate. If it's not accurate it won't work. It won't be... fulfilling

LEAH: (*gives him the bag*) Right, sorry. OK

TOM: Thank you. Thank you for...thank you

LEAH: You don't have to thank me

TOM: No, right, of course

Tom sits and gestures for her to sit too. She does. Her body language is sexual.

So what did you have today?

LEAH: Have?

TOM: At school?

LEAH: Oh, right. Um, maths, Eng/lish

TOM: Maths you say?

LEAH: Yeah

TOM: What were you doing?

LEAH: (*thinks*) Times tables

TOM: Times tables? You're in the top set

LEAH: Am I? Right. Oh shit, um...quadratic equations

TOM: And?

LEAH: And?

TOM: How did you find it?

LEAH: Quite tough

TOM: And English, 'Of Mice and Men' right?

LEAH: *(brightening)* Yeah

TOM: Have you read it?

LEAH: Yeah, *(genuinely)* I *really* have

TOM: Good.

LEAH: *(gaining confidence)* We were looking at the theme of friendship. Our homework is to write an essay on the relationship between George and Lennie – is their friendship fully reciprocal?

TOM: And is it? Do you think?

LEAH: You can argue it either way

TOM: But in your opinion

LEAH: In my experience one person always needs the other more

TOM: I see.

Pause.

Undo your tie a little, and your top button

LEAH: Sure *(Leah does as requested)* Anything else?

TOM: No, that'll be fine.

LEAH: (*standing and starting to roll her skirt*) I can / roll my skir / t

TOM: No thank you

She sits. They look out. A moment passes.

Any plans for the weekend? Are you seeing that boy… Rory?

LEAH: (*slowly*) Yeah, yeah on Saturday

TOM: Really?

LEAH: Yeah, we're going / to the

TOM: To the cinema and then for a pizza, you'll have a chicken supreme but substitute the onions for sweetcorn and add extra cheese, you'll wear your skinny black jeans, converse trainers and your off the shoulder guns n' roses T-shirt – you'll first come down in your tiny black crop top but I'll tell you that you are absolutely not going out in that thing and you'll change, you'll see that new film 'What's Love Got To Do With It? as you love emotional films and Shazad Latif, and that boy Rory will sit through anything if it means he can put his hands on your breasts – I've seen him do it outside our front door when he kisses you goodnight, it takes all my restraint not to come out and throw a bucket of water over him but it's actually very normal and he is really rather sweet, when you get in you'll still want to be cross with me but you won't be able to because you'll want to tell me all about it, you can talk more easily to me than to your mother, I'll raise my eyebrows at the appropriate moments and laugh when you regurgitate his jokes and be impressed that he paid for everything and then we'll discuss the film, who was good, who wasn't, what the director was trying to say and this will inspire us to put a film on, we'll choose an oldie - maybe an Audrey Hepburn – and we'll lip-sync the famous lines and drink tea and eat biscuits until I notice you're falling asleep and then I'll suggest you go up to bed and you'll say good idea Pops and as you walk past me you'll kiss me on the forehead and say love you

He stops, regains control of himself and looks out. Silence.

TOM: Sorry

LEAH: I recognise you now, from the appeals on TV and the newspapers

TOM: Do you?

LEAH: Yeah

TOM: But it was six months ago…more

LEAH: I read an interview you did… You were the last one to see her

TOM: Yes. I dropped her off for school, just round the corner so she could walk in with her friends. She never arrived. Never met them

Pause

LEAH: I love Audrey Hepburn *(pause)* 'I ain't dirty, I washed me face an' 'ands before I come I did'

Tom looks at her. Beat.

TOM: I think this was a mistake

He exits. Leah stands and watches him go. As she is about to leave she notices his wallet has fallen from his pocket, she runs to see if she can see him but he is gone.

LEAH: Shit

She picks up the wallet and her rucksack and leaves.

SCENE 2

Kitchen. Gill sips a glass of wine. She glances at her watch and starts to put on her coat.

TOM: Gill?

Tom enters taking off his coat.

GILL: Just caught me

TOM: Where you off to?

GILL: Church

TOM: Again?

GILL: Yeah

TOM: *(nodding)* Right

GILL: How was today?

TOM: Fine. You?

GILL: Better. I survived Year nine History with Dillon Hopkins and Karl Whittaker *(beat)* I came to find you at lunchtime but you weren't in your classroom

TOM: I went off site. I'm afraid I succumbed… to a cigarette

She nods.

GILL: I did you a salad. It's in the fridge

TOM: Great. Lovely. Thank you

Beat. She hands him an envelope from Amazon.

GILL: This came for you

TOM: Ah

GILL: It feels like a CD…?

TOM: Yeah, I just fancied it

She nods.

GILL: What's on it?

TOM: Just music

She holds his gaze. Beat.

That song, she sang at the concert, you know/the one

GILL: I know which one

TOM: Any calls? Messages?

Gill shakes her head.

Stupid question

Gill rubs his back and squeezes his hands.

GILL: I can hang on, if you want to come with me. Might help

TOM: No

GILL: Tom

TOM: Gill, if it makes you feel better then go but I'm not coming

GILL: Please

Silence. She nods. He looks up and sees Matilda – a soft toy rabbit – sitting on the kitchen counter.

TOM: What's Matilda doing down here?

GILL: I just...

He nods.

TOM: We should keep her in Sophie's room. So the smell of food doesn't

GILL: *(cutting him off)* Yeah, I'll put it back

TOM: No, no, you go, I'll...

GILL: It's how her head used to smell when she was a baby

Tom looks away.

    If you close your eyes

TOM: Gill please

GILL: I need to

TOM: It's been a long day

GILL: Fine

She finishes up her wine.

TOM: *(indicating the wine)* God's OK with that is he?

GILL: *(hurt)* I'm trying my best

TOM: If he's not there's a fair few glasses to atone for

GILL: I'm not listening to this

Gill starts to exit.

TOM: Gill, I'm sorry, I'm sorry love

Gill leaves.

>Shit

Moments pass.

Tom picks up the envelope, opens it and looks at the cd – the song begins to play. He looks at Matilda for a long time. The door opens and Gill enters. They look at each other.

GILL: Let's not be those people

SCENE 3

A bedsit. Mark lifts weights. Leah enters. He looks her up and down. She starts to get undressed.

MARK: You look a state

LEAH: I know

MARK: Fat thighs

LEAH: Yeah

MARK: He liked it though?

LEAH: Yeah, seemed to

MARK: Yeah?

LEAH: Yeah, I just had to sit there, laugh at his jokes, smile

MARK: One of those

LEAH: Yeah

MARK: Corporate?

LEAH: Yeah. Someone was leaving the department

MARK: And? *(beat)* Come on Leah

LEAH: We met outside the bar – like you said – he took my hands, leant in, checked I knew who I was and what I should do

MARK: Good

LEAH: Then he lead me inside, kept me in the corner, told them I was a nurse – just finished a twelve hour shift so not too expect too much from me – it was a joke, I laughed

MARK: Where did he put his hands?

LEAH: *(wary)* On my thigh

MARK: Beyond the scar?

LEAH: No

MARK: Sure?

LEAH: Sure

MARK: Swear?

LEAH: Yes

MARK: Good, carry on

He smiles, she relaxes

LEAH: He brushed his fingers

MARK: Leah, do it properly

LEAH: *(taking her time, sexy, moving towards him)* He brushed his fingers across my lips, slipped his arm around my waist, kissed me on the cheek as we got into the cab

MARK: Did he want it?

LEAH: Yeah

Mark smiles, puts his hands on her. During the next they move to the floor – him between her legs

MARK: Did he ask for it?

LEAH: No

MARK: So how d'you know?

LEAH: I could tell

MARK: You can do better than that

LEAH: He leant over, in the cab, breathed me in

MARK: And?

LEAH: Touched my thigh again *(Mark touches her thigh)*

MARK: So what did you do?

LEAH: Smiled

MARK: And

LEAH: He moved it higher *(he moves his hand higher)*

MARK: Above the scar?

LEAH: No, not that high

MARK: Right. *(beat)* So you?

LEAH: Smiled, shook my head, got my phone out

MARK: And he just stopped?

He removes his hand, sits up.

LEAH: Yeah

MARK: Good girl

She pulls him back to kiss him.

MARK: Stand up

LEAH: What?

She starts to sit up

MARK: You know how this works

LEAH: Yeah but I've told you what ha / ppened

MARK: You said he was a perv

LEAH: I didn't say that

MARK: He 'breathed' you in?! (*He pulls her roughly to standing*) Had his hand on your thigh

LEAH: Yeah, that's allowed, as long as he stops when I tell him to

MARK: He wanted it

LEAH: You told me to make him want it, that's the point

MARK: Yeah

LEAH: So he'd book me /again

MARK: Yeah, but what I don't know is 'did you'?

LEAH: No, it's just a job

MARK: Yeah, s'posed / to be

LEAH: That you asked me to do

MARK: Correct. But I don't know what goes on in there *(he pokes his finger at the side of her head)* do I?

LEAH: No but. Mark, I don't want to do this anymore

MARK: *(sharp)* Then how are we gonna pay for everything? Mm?

Leah shrugs.

Do you wanna go back to that hostel? Do you? Do you?

LEAH: I don't/ know

MARK: What do you mean you don't fucking know? You should thank me. I've sorted you an easy life

LEAH: I know

MARK: Some blokes would make you work three jobs, cleaning and shit

LEAH: I know, I'm grateful but

MARK: But what?

LEAH: -

MARK: I do it all... I found that agency, signed you up, uploaded your profile, I filter your jobs, sort out all your money. All you have to do is fucking dress up, show-up and smile

LEAH: Yeah

MARK: Yeah right. But this bloke tonight was a perv, right? He overstepped the mark?

LEAH: No, he was sad

MARK: Sad?

LEAH: Yeah, he seemed sad

MARK: No emotions Leah, remember?

LEAH: Yeah

MARK: That's one of our rules

LEAH: Yeah

MARK: *(grabbing her face to make her look at him)* Oi, you're doing it for us, for me, not for them

LEAH: I know

MARK: They're just dirty bastards with lots of money and fuck all personality

LEAH: *(resigned)* Yeah

MARK: A little louder please

LEAH: Yes

MARK: Stand still

LEAH: Oh for God's sake Mark

Mark looks at her.

> Sorry, sorry, sorry, sorry

MARK: You know, you know I can't enjoy it if I haven't checked

LEAH: I know

Leah stands as Mark checks behind her neck and under her finger nails.

>Why don't you trust me?

MARK: Experience

LEAH: But I've never / done anything

MARK: Makes no difference.

LEAH: Follow me, watch if you want

MARK: *(laughs)* I don't want to watch, I like... That's part of it. *(beat)* Take this off *(he indicates her cardigan)*

LEAH: Mark

MARK: Don't. Make. Me. Feel. Like. Shit.

Leah does so. Silence as he looks at her. He starts to laugh and hit his head with his hands

MARK: Your strap's twisted

LEAH: What?

MARK: Your strap. Why?

LEAH: I don't know

MARK: Why you lying to me Leah?

LEAH: I'm not

MARK: Shut it

He begins to sniff down her body.

LEAH: See?

He continues to sniff

MARK: Stand still

LEAH: Mark, he didn't do anything

Silence. He continues to sniff

MARK: Get your knickers off

LEAH: What?

MARK: I can smell him all over you. Get in there and get your FUCKING knickers off.

LEAH: Please

MARK: I have to check inside you

Leah is frozen. He pulls her wrist roughly and she goes. He follows.

SCENE 4

London. A bridge. Leah enters. She wears the same clothes as in the previous scene but with trainers and a parker. She is crying. She looks around then stands looking out over the bridge. Tom enters. He approaches slowly, making sure that it's her.

TOM: Sorry I'm late, I couldn't get away, my wife wouldn't go to bed

Leah nods but does not turn around. She is trying to get herself together

> It's an odd time to meet... two am... not that I'm complaining, I'm extremely grateful... could I have my wallet?

Leah turns wiping away her tears

> Oh my God

LEAH: I'm fine

TOM: Right. Was it a client?

LEAH: What?

TOM: That upset you? That hurt you?

LEAH: No, no, God no

TOM: Are you sure?

Tom nods

> Sure?

LEAH: *(nods)* This was my fault

TOM: Right. Can I do/anything

LEAH: Look, I'm fine

TOM: *(stepping back)* Ok, ok...

LEAH: I upset him, make him angry so... He wants to hear... about the men, and then he...

Beat. Leah looks at him quickly, then looks out. Tom nods. Fiddles in his pocket and brings out a handkerchief and offers it to Leah.

TOM: Here

She smiles. Takes it. Composes herself

LEAH: Sorry it's so late

He shakes his head

LEAH: In the day I can't always get away but at night he drinks 'til he's out of it so *(beat)* Sorry

TOM: No need. I'm just glad to be getting it back

LEAH: *(getting the wallet out of her pocket)* It's all there

TOM: I didn't imagine it wouldn't be

Beat. He rummages in the wallet, pulls out a twenty pound note.

Here

LEAH: What's that for?

TOM: For you, to say thank you

LEAH: For not nicking it?

TOM: I didn't mean it like that

LEAH: What do you think I am?

TOM: I... sorry

He puts the money away.

LEAH: I thought it was only Paddington who had a label

TOM: Sorry?

LEAH: If this bear is lost please return to

TOM: Oh, yes. My wife bought me the wallet, put that inside. She knows what I'm like losing things

Leah nods, looks down at the water.

LEAH: It would be so easy

TOM: You wouldn't do it though... would you?

Beat. Tom looks out.

TOM: I think about it

She looks at him.

LEAH: *(shocked)* Really?

TOM: Maybe

LEAH: Scared?

TOM: Are you?

LEAH: No

TOM: Be cold

LEAH: And wet

They both laugh.

It takes two to three minutes... to drown

He considers.

TOM: Unless you're a world-class swimmer, or an athlete, or just really good at holding your breath

LEAH: Are you?

TOM: No

LEAH: Your involuntary nervous system kicks in. Your body goes into overdrive. When the brain dies, it empties its full load of endorphins, your brain is literally flooded with them, you go out on a massive high. Like you've just taken a bag of E

TOM: That sounds rather nice

LEAH: *(glancing at him)* I read that.

TOM: Look, um... Do you want me to stay?

LEAH: No, I'm fine

TOM: Sure? It's just... my wife, she'll panic if she wakes up and / I'm not

LEAH: It's OK

TOM: Right. You promise

LEAH: I promise. *(beat)* It was nice meeting you again

Tom leaves. Leah climbs back on to the bridge. Tom glances back, sees Leah, and rushes across to grab hold of her

TOM: Oh my God. No, no, please... please

LEAH: What? I'm just dangling my legs

TOM: What?

LEAH: I'm dangling my legs, it feels nice

TOM: Oh my God.

LEAH: It's OK

TOM: I'm sorry

After a moment Tom climbs on to bridge next to Leah.

LEAH: What are you doing? I thought you had to go?

TOM: I'm dangling my legs. *(beat)* You're right, it does feel nice

Beat

LEAH: Is it 'cos I look like her?

TOM: What?

LEAH: Your daughter? ...Sarah? Sophia?

TOM: Sophie.

LEAH: Sophie. *(beat)* Oh God, sorry, that was rude, I didn't / mean to

TOM: It's OK

LEAH: I can't imagine... what you must have / been through...

TOM: No.

Beat.

LEAH: You do know you can't jump now? It would be hypocritical

Tom smirks.

TOM: I see

Pause.

LEAH: You'd never have jumped anyway

Tom looks at her

 Because you're not sure if she's dead

TOM: -

LEAH: You still hope

TOM: Do I?

A beat. Leah looks out. He smiles.

 So what does that say about you?

LEAH: I'm hopeless

Beat. She smiles, he does not. She swings her legs back over the bridge.

 I think I might leave it 'til tomorrow

She climbs off the bridge.

TOM: Same time, same place?

LEAH: I'll try

Leah leaves. He watches her go.

SCENE 5

London. Sophie's bedroom.

GILL: So tell me how it was?

TOM: Not like she made it sound. I didn't touch her. I just wanted to talk

GILL: They say it's a 'safeguarding issue', you're not allowed to go into school

TOM: I just wanted to talk / to her

GILL: Talk? Talk? She's what – a fourteen, fifteen year old girl? Outside the lesson what the hell have you got to talk to her about?

TOM: Gill, you know. Come on, you, you must understand

GILL: I'm trying Tom but you need to explain it to me

TOM: I just wanted to be back in Sophie's world, to know about the things she would know about. Do you know, for the first time in five years, I don't know who's at number one?

Gill audibly exhales with frustration

I don't know what is happening to me. I can't function without her. My mind won't sleep, if I'm awake I'm bombarded with images of her strung up in some warehouse or locked in a cupboard, or bruised or raped or stabbed or... and if I sleep, it's the same – or worse. Except sometimes, in my dreams, I *am* her and I'm being chased and I'm screaming for 'Dad' but Dad never comes and I'm tied up and hit and... and the only thought that keeps me going is that 'Dad wouldn't let this happen to me, that any moment he'll be here and he'll stop him, just as soon as he realises that I'm missing. But Dad doesn't come and Dad doesn't come and eventually my hope dies and I become aware that he's not going to come. And I have to accept that this is it. That this is my life now. And I have to forget Dad.' *(beat)* So no, like you say, perhaps I'm not in my right mind

GILL: So that's why you… touched her?

TOM: *(quietly)* I did not

GILL: Sue says that's what she's said…

TOM: I know

GILL: She couldn't be any more specific, shouldn't even have told me that much

TOM: I don't know / what to

GILL: I mean it's not the first time you've been accused of being 'tactile'

TOM: Bloody hell Gill, that was yeas ago – a pat on the head, you know it / was

GILL: But – this time – you don't deny you kept her, this girl, behind after class, and asked her 'questions of a personal nature'.

TOM: You see, I don't know what that means. What does that actually mean?

GILL: That's what I'm asking – what did you say?

TOM: We just chatted – how were things at school? At home? *(beat)* Boys?

GILL: What kind of questions about boys?

TOM: Oh for... nothing invasive just... Look, she wasn't her normal self, I just wanted to make sure everything was ok. To protect her. She likes, liked, me and trusted me

GILL: So why report you? Tom? That's what I don't understand

TOM: I don't know. Maybe I kept her for too long, asked too many questions, was a bit too intense. She's a teenage girl. She doesn't realise the impact of what she's saying. I wouldn't...

GILL: What? What wouldn't you do?

TOM: Anything. You know I'd never do anything to a child

GILL: Yes, I do, I do I do know that. Do I?

TOM: Yes / of course

GILL: But our daughter is missing and you're being accused of being inappropriate with / a teenage girl

TOM: For God's sake

GILL: I need to know

TOM: What?

GILL: I need to know / if you

TOM: No / no

GILL: If you touched Sophie

TOM: No

GILL: Perhaps something she misinterpreted? Everyone will think it

TOM: But not you/ not you

GILL: SHE'S GONE

TOM: I know.

GILL: And you think you're the only one suffering, trying to adjust, trying to be normal but you're not, you're fucking not. Everyone's waiting, waiting for me to break. I see them at school in huddles, furtive glances – am I still bothering to dye my hair, iron my clothes, clean my fucking teeth. And I shut them out, push them away and then I come home to you, to you, to cling to you but you're… We should be together but we're not because you're… off being inappropriate with a teenage girl. And I can't help thinking… Did I miss something? Did I not want to see? You were always close, closer than us almost. You'd stay up watching films, chatting and what else? She was becoming a woman, oh God. And I can't, I can't, I can't get it out of my head. And I won't, I will not be one of those women who refuses to see it, who turns a blind eye

TOM: To what?

GILL: You know what

TOM: How can you think that?

GILL: How can I not?

TOM: She didn't take any of her things

GILL: You see you say that like it proves something but it doesn't

TOM: Someone's got her Gill

GILL: How can you be so sure? Or are you trying to convince me because of what you've done? I can't do this, I can't

She leaves. Tom remains.

SCENE 6

Bedsit. Leah is on all fours, Mark crouches in front of her applying her lipstick. When he finishes he stands and clicks his fingers. On this command Leah stands

MARK: Beautiful. Give us a spin

Dutifully she spins.

    And another

She spins again

    Did I choose well?

LEAH: *(looking at the dress, nods)* Yeah, thank you

MARK: It was expensive

LEAH: I know

He clicks his fingers and Leah returns to all fours

MARK: So, it's Mr theatre and drinks tonight

LEAH: Yeah

MARK: Second time in a month. He must like you

LEAH: Maybe

MARK: Definitely, I'd say

LEAH: Mark, don't start

MARK: *(softly)* I'm not, I'm proud of you. You're gorgeous, do you know that?

LEAH: I'm tired, Mark

MARK: Yeah, about last night, I was just... you're such a pleaser, people take advantage. Do you forgive me?

LEAH: Yeah

MARK: Right

LEAH: I'd rather not go tonight

MARK: Yeah, I know, but it's just for now, for us. 'Til we're back on our feet *(beat)* Pretend this is all for me

LEAH: It could be

MARK: Nah Leah, nah... pretend

LEAH: OK

He clicks and Leah moves to crouching

MARK: I've got something for you

LEAH: What? ...You didn't need to

MARK: I know

He pulls out a curly wurly.

Da-da! Curly wurly!

She laughs. He holds it out to her, she goes to take it but he pulls it away.

MARK: *(playing)* Come on, beg... You know you want it

Leah puts out her tongue like a dog and begins to chase the curlywurly Mark dangles in front of her

MARK: Come on, good girl, come and get the curlywurly, come on, come on, chase, chase it, chase, chase, chase. Come on, you know you want it – woohoo *(he mimes it being his penis)* – come and get it

He throws it on the floor

Go on

Leah runs to pick it up and begins to open it

Uh, uh, uh. *(he takes it from her)* Make it last. Go slow *(he opens it for her and puts it to her lips)* Suck it

He watches her

Lucky bastard. Be on your guard tonight, yeah?

LEAH: Course

Beat.

MARK: Have we got time?

LEAH: *(glancing at her watch)* No

MARK: Ooo, I think so. *(he looks at his penis)* I'm ready

LEAH: Please Mark

MARK: It's aching

LEAH: Please, I'll be late

MARK: I did buy you a curlywurly... I want to make up

LEAH: We have

MARK: I mean properly *(he motions toward the bed)* I want to say sorry

LEAH: You've said it

MARK: Leah I need this

LEAH: It'll hurt

MARK: Don't be difficult

LEAH: I'm still sore.

MARK: I'll be quick

LEAH: What you did to me yesterday

MARK: I want him to smell me on you

LEAH: No, Mark

MARK: It'll make him horny

LEAH: I don't want to

MARK: It'll turn him on

LEAH: No

MARK: Trust me, Leah

LEAH: I said no

MARK: Stop being such a fucking *(he slaps her face)* prick-tease.

He picks her up roughly

>Come on. You can keep your dress on

SCENE 7

Lounge. Gill zips up a packed suitcase. Tom enters.

TOM: I can come back later if you haven't finished

GILL: It's fine. I'm done now

He nods, goes to speak.

Don't make this any harder than it is

Silence.

TOM: Is there anything I can say?

GILL: -

TOM: Where will you be?

GILL: Tom

TOM: In an emergency

GILL: My mother's

TOM: I've done nothing wrong

GILL: It was Emily, Sophie's friend. What were you thinking?

TOM: I've n / ot

GILL: She's not been in school

TOM: -

GILL: Do you know what you've done?

TOM: I know what I've been accused of. There's a difference

GILL: Is there? *(beat)* You're being investigated

TOM: It's not an investigation unless they decide to formally suspend me

GILL: Which they might

TOM: But Gill / I

GILL: There's already abuse on the Facebook page

TOM: Please stay

GILL: I can't. I just need a bit of time. A week or / two

TOM: Please.

Beat. She starts to leave.

    At least wait until you're sober

GILL: How dare you

TOM: That wasn't a judgement.

She's gone.

SCENE 8

Leah in the park, she looks around, waiting for someone. She holds a plastic bag containing two portions of chips. Mark appears. She doesn't see him. He approaches her and squeezes her around the waist. She smiles and turns around, is shocked to see Mark.

LEAH: Mark?

MARK: What? Been found out?

LEAH: No... no. I

MARK: Wanted to find out why you were in such a hurry

LEAH: W... I just... I wasn't... I... This is personal, it's...

MARK: *(turning to her)* Personal? I'm your boyfriend

LEAH: That doesn't mean you own me sorry, sorry, sorry

MARK: What are you saying Leah?

LEAH: I'm just... I just fancied some chips... and a walk

MARK: Right

LEAH: I wanted some air

MARK: Away from me?

LEAH: No... well – yes... but not

MARK: Because I'm too much sometimes

LEAH: No, Mark... I didn't say that... just... Stop it

MARK: Stop what?

LEAH: Putting words in my mouth. Just stop. I come here sometimes, it's... somewhere I come to... think about stuff. I thought you were going to be at the job centre so / I

MARK: Why do you treat me like a twat Leah?

LEAH: *(stroking his back)* I don't

MARK: I think you forget about me when you go out with these men, eh?

LEAH: Course I don't

MARK: You know you're just a whore, right?

LEAH: *(she turns from him, resigned. Quietly)* Yeah

MARK: Correction, a whore who never takes her knickers down

She nods.

Right?

LEAH: Yes, right

MARK: I *let* you do this prick-teasing job because it turns me on, thinking about those sad bastards coming in their pants at the thought / of you

LEAH: That is disgusting, it's not like that

MARK: Of course it's fucking 'like that', don't be so naïve. *(beat)* But it's okay Lea, you see I like them looking at you, brushing against you, touching your leg, kissing you even, because it's only me you sleep with,

>it's only me right? They're not real. You hate them. *(beat)* But I *am* real and you're mine. Aren't you?

LEAH: Yeah

MARK: And you wouldn't fuck around with anyone else would you?

She shakes her head. Tom appears, he hangs back, unseen by Leah and Mark.

>Because that really would take the piss, wouldn't it?

She nods.

>Because no-one else would be with you, would they? No-one else would put up with the way you are?

LEAH: No

MARK: Good

He kisses her roughly

>I'm sorry. But I won't be made a fool of. *(suddenly remembers and looks at his watch)* Shit. I'll call you when I'm out. *(beat)* Enjoy your chips

He exits. Leah watches him go. After a pause, Tom steps forward. Leah is embarrassed as she guesses he saw some of the exchange. During the following few lines Leah is distracted, worried that Mark hasn't gone - she keeps checking.

LEAH: Hi, I got them

TOM: So I see.

LEAH: I love chips, they always taste better when you eat them outside, don't you think?

TOM: Yeah, I know what you /mean

LEAH: It's like the air reacts with them and brings out the flavour, maybe, before salt was… invented the air from the sea made them salty, so that's why they came to be known as something you eat by the sea, with salt

TOM: For someone so intelligent, you don't half talk a lot of shit

LEAH: *(defensive)* Cheers.

They sit.

TOM: *(taking bag)* Come on, what've we got?

LEAH: Just chips. That's right isn't it? It's what we had last time

TOM: Perfect. And… *(he pulls a bottle of champagne out of his bag)*

LEAH: Champagne?

TOM: She would have been sixteen today / so I thought we should celebrate

LEAH: Shit, Tom I / didn't

TOM: Shh, just have a drink. I've already had a couple, should've waited but…

They both take a swig then begin eating chips. Tom drinks more than he eats. Time passes.

LEAH: Oh for fuck sake, yes that was Mark. *(beat)* He's not always like that

TOM: Wh / y?

LEAH: Don't say it

TOM: Right. Sorry

LEAH: You remind me of my Dad. *(beat)* He used to do that. Just sit there oozing his disapproval

TOM: Sorry

LEAH: *(cracking a smile)* I like it.

He looks at her. They eat.

TOM: I think I'm going to lose my job

LEAH: -

TOM: I've been formally suspended pending an investigation and a disciplinary hearing *(beat)* The girl made a statement. Said I touched her inappropriately, that I was coming on to her. *(beat)* She's lying

He looks at Leah, she nods.

> I denied it in my interview. But they looked at me like I could have done it. They said 'you're not on trial' but I was. Obviously

Pause.

> And Gill's not come back. It's been a week now

LEAH: Have you spoken?

TOM: Once

LEAH: And?

TOM: She'd just found out about you

LEAH: Found out what?

TOM: The other day, when you met me at the tube station... One of her friends saw me with you... They thought you were Sophie

LEAH: Shit

TOM: Rang her

LEAH: Shit

TOM: She went berserk

LEAH: What did you say?

TOM: That you were a friend

LEAH: And?

TOM: She hung up

LEAH: I'm so so / rry

TOM: Don't be. It's not your fault

He shakes his head, smiles at her. They look out. Moments pass.

    Why Lea?

LEAH: Why what?

TOM: Mark

She looks out.

LEAH: He held my hand after the funeral

TOM: -

Throughout the next section Tom drinks.

LEAH: Mum's funeral

TOM: I'm so sorry

LEAH: Don't be. She was... well

Beat. Tom waits.

Mum was dead, I was a mess, Mark was... kind

TOM: What about your Dad?

LEAH: Left when I was eleven. *(beat)* One day I came home from school and all his stuff had gone. Everything. *(beat)* Then two months later Darren moved in to 'look after us'. *(beat)* At the start I still saw Dad, every Saturday, he'd take me somewhere, the history museum, the zoo, McDonalds

Tom smiles.

Then that first Summer holiday after he left I was allowed to go with him to Scotland for a week – place called Portsoy, right by the sea *(she smiles at the memory)*. Then, on the way home, he told me he was going to move up there, with a woman he'd met

TOM: Oh Le / ah

LEAH: Said I could visit every holiday and that he'd come down and see me but I told him he could piss off. *(beat)* He used to ring me, really late at night, usually drunk, sometimes crying but I was so angry with him... Then one time Mum heard and she took my phone away so he couldn't call anymore... *(beat)* Then we moved to Croydon, she didn't tell him our new address and that was it.

TOM: Shit

LEAH: That was when Darren...

TOM: What?

LEAH: And I thought, this is my punishment. *(beat)* When Mum died I was nineteen, I thought Dad'll come back now. I'd planned out everything I was going to say. But he never came

Pause.

After her funeral I stayed by her grave. Waited for hours and hours, I was so sure. *(beat)* That's when Mark showed up. I'd seen him in the pubs and that but...

Checks to see if Tom is with her.

I didn't see him arrive, I just suddenly felt this person take my hand *(beat)* Stupid really, I always knew he was a twat

Pause. Tom offers her the champagne. She takes it.

TOM: So why stay?

LEAH: I love him

Tom nods. They eat chips.

TOM: These are good. Salty

Leah smiles. Moments pass

> I did touch that girl

Leah looks at him.

> I stroked her face. *(beat)* It wasn't sexual. She was crying and I stroked her face

Tom stands.

> Sod it, dance with me

LEAH: No

TOM: Come on just one dance - it's her birthday

LEAH: *(still sitting)* No, I can't, I'll feel stupid

TOM: *(pulling her up)* Come on, this is a party Leah

LEAH: I have to go and meet Mark soon

TOM: He's not invited

LEAH: Fine. Look, I can't hang around for ages

TOM: I'm having a party, it would be rude of you to leave

LEAH: Sorry

During the next Mark enters unseen by Leah and Tom, he watches.

TOM: *(stops dancing and looks at her sincerely, his pain burning through)* Don't be sorry, she's sixteen today. It's a big one, sixteen. She's a grown-up now. She can leave home, have sex, drive a moped. It would be wrong not to mark the occasion. *(They begin to dance)*

MARK: Surprise

They freeze.

LEAH: I thought we were meeting later?

MARK: Wanted to see who was getting the other portion

LEAH: What?

MARK: Saw you buy two portions of chips

He looks at Tom.

Is this the friend you were telling me about? What did you say his name was?

LEAH: Mark, it's not

MARK: What's his name Leah?

LEAH: Tom

MARK: *(going over to Tom)* Hello mate, I'm Mark, nice to meet you

TOM: *(shaking his hand)* Hi

MARK: Leah's told me all about you

TOM: *(glancing at Leah)* Has she?

MARK: *(smiles)* Yeah. Great when you can put a face to a name

TOM: Yes.

MARK: Anyway, I'm gonna have to take this little one *(pulls her to him a little too roughly)* – we've got somewhere to be ain't we Lea?

LEAH: Yeah

TOM: *(gathering things)* Of course. *(awkward beat. To Leah)* OK?

Leah nods quickly.

    (to Mark) Nice to meet you

Tom exits.

MARK: 'OK'?

LEAH: Just what people say

MARK: *(he nods)* Hmm. *(beat)* Looks like I missed the party

LEAH: What?

MARK: Champagne?

LEAH: Please Mark

MARK: Please Mark what? He's the pervert that got you to dress up as a school girl?

LEAH: Yeah, but he's not a per/vert

MARK: Was this a freebie? Are you fucking him?

LEAH: Mark

MARK: Are you?

LEAH: Stop it

MARK: I mean you look very young, I know he likes that

LEAH: Stop it

MARK: Well, yes or no?

LEAH: He's my friend

MARK: That's not an answer Leah

LEAH: -

MARK: Answer me

LEAH: NO I'M NOT

MARK: DON'T YOU SHOUT AT ME. *(beat)* Fucking chips and champagne! What am I meant to think? Eh? Eh?

LEAH: He's sad

MARK: Sad?

LEAH: Yeah, about his daughter. Look, we just talk, that's all it is

MARK: Right. And he's happy with that?

LEAH: Yes

MARK: Right

LEAH: It helps

MARK: Helps who?

LEAH: Him, me

MARK: You?!

LEAH: Yes. I like talking to him

MARK: You've got me

LEAH: I know but it's different

MARK: Now we're getting to it, you want to try something different

LEAH: *(getting flustered)* N... he's older

MARK: More experienced

LEAH: I'm not talking about that / he's

MARK: What else is there?

LEAH: He's like my Dad

MARK: So you want to shag a man just like him?

LEAH: No. He just likes me

MARK: *(scoffing)* You what? *(beat)* You think he 'likes you for you?' You're a nothing person. You know that, you told me that. Even your mum and dad fucked off. You're fuckable, that's it

LEAH: Sorry

MARK: Didn't hear you

LEAH: Sorry

MARK: Only *I* know the real you and, like a mug, I still stay. I don't fucking know why. FUCKING HELL Leah, why is being with you so fucking difficult

He takes out a stanley knife.

I think I need to do another one

LEAH: No Mark, please

MARK: Last time is just a scar now, isn't it?

LEAH: I know what I am, I swear

MARK: I know sweetheart. But it's not for you, it's for anyone who goes too near you

LEAH: They won't

MARK: We can't be sure though, can we?

LEAH: Yes we can

MARK: Roll it up

LEAH: Please Mark

MARK: Roll it

She rolls up her skirt to reveal the word 'whore' cut into the top of her thigh.

See sweetheart, it's faded. Come on

He walks off, she follows.

SCENE 9

Outside Tom's house. Late. Leah sits in the half light. She wears the same clothes as Scene 8 but with the addition of a parker. She has a rucksack stuffed full which is beside her. She has a black eye.

Gill enters with a bottle of champagne. She sees Leah who has her back to her. Gill stops, stunned.

GILL: *(almost a whisper)* Sophie *(starting to run)* Sophie!

She runs to throw her arms around her, Leah turns.

Gill releases a huge sob of revulsion, shock and pain.

> You, you

LEAH: *(stands)* Oh God I'm sorry, I'm so sorry

Gill vomits.

> I shouldn't have come, I don't know what I was thinking.

GILL: *(she starts to laugh)* It's a joke, it's a fucking joke. You look so much like her. It's sick. *(beat)*. You know it's her birthday today of course you do he tells you everything I'm sure I'm a fucking bitch right?

LEAH: No

GILL: No!

She snorts, puts her face in her hands.

> Has he stood you up?

LEAH: He didn't know I was coming

70

GILL: A surprise visit. What are you wearing under there?

LEAH: -

GILL: Sorry. Sorry, I just don't know what to say to you

LEAH: I'm / not

GILL: Thought maybe, maybe I'd made a mistake and you can't really blame me I mean the evidence would suggest but, no, I thought no, I've been hasty, disloyal – a bitch? So I thought bottle of champagne – we always had one, on her birthday, not her obviously, just him and I, after she'd gone to bed. He always used to say that it should be the mum who got presents and cards on their child's birthday – that they should be the one being celebrated for the monumental effort it took to bring their offspring into the world. And so that's what he did, when she'd gone to bed, he would give me a present and a card and we'd drink a bottle of champagne and he would toast me. *(beat)* And I remembered that today and I thought... that man, that man who did that could not and would not hurt our daughter, he couldn't and so I came to *(she looks at Leah)* and I find you here and I, I DON'T FUCKING KNOW ANYMORE

LEAH: He really is a good man

GILL: *(laughs)* Is he? Is he? *(beat)* But why you? Why didn't he fight harder for us?

LEAH: He's just trying to cope

GILL: Sleeping with you?

LEAH: Talking to me

GILL: *(she laughs)* So you're just here for cocoa and a bedtime story? Give me a break.

LEAH: I don't know what else to say

Gill gives Leah the champagne.

GILL: Nothing

Gill leaves. Leah watches her go.

Moments pass. Tom enters. He sees Leah.

TOM: Leah?

As he moves closer to her he sees the bruises.

I heard voices – oh God, look at you

She pulls back from his touch.

LEAH: Careful

TOM: Was it…?

LEAH: Yeah

TOM: I'm so s / orry

LEAH: It's not your fault. Please *(she shakes her head)*

TOM: I should've stayed

Leah shrugs.

LEAH: I hope you don't mind me just turning up like this

TOM: *(he smiles)* Mi casa, tu casa

LEAH: ?

TOM: My home is your home

Beat.

LEAH: Your wife was here

TOM: -

LEAH: She thought I was Sophie

TOM: Shit

LEAH: Brought a bottle of champagne

TOM: Shit

LEAH: She wasn't too pleased to see me

TOM: No

LEAH: She said she'd thought you could celebrate Sophie's birthday like you used to

Beat.

She thinks you're sleeping with me

TOM: God's sake

LEAH: I told her *(shakes her head, he nods)* Sorry. If I've made things more difficult

TOM: Don't be ridiculous. *(beat)* Stay with me Lea

She looks at him.

You deserve better

LEAH: I don't

TOM: You could stop the escorting. I'll take care of you. I'd like to take care of you. *(beat)* Leah?

Pause.

LEAH: You really are a good man. I told her that

TOM: Did you hear what I said?

Leah nods.

    Come and live with me

LEAH: I can't

TOM: Why not? It makes sense

LEAH: 'Cos you're from a different world. You're not like us, you're not like me

TOM: I'm not asking for anything Lea

LEAH: I know that

TOM: I'm just saying… I have a big house with a spare room and hot water and food and it's safe. I / won't

LEAH: I don't deserve it

TOM: Le / ah

LEAH: You don't know what I'm really like, what things I've done. If you did, you wouldn't look at me

TOM: That's not true

LEAH: Well

TOM: Just give it a chance

Leah looks at Tom. He nods.

> Arnica

LEAH: Sorry?

TOM: It's what you put on bruises to reduce swelling and colour. I have some inside

She looks at him. He smiles.

> Now there's an offer you can't refuse

She smiles weakly.

> I promise I will never let anyone hurt you again

Beat.

> Come on, let's go in

She goes in. He follows.

INTERVAL

SCENE 10

Dining room. Tom sits at the table reading a book – 'To Kill A Mockingbird' – Leah enters. She wears one of Tom's t-shirts and his dressing gown.

TOM: Hello you

LEAH: Morning

TOM: Good sleep?

LEAH: Yeah, lovely

She smiles. He looks at her and very gently touches the bruise around her eye.

TOM: Looks better this morning

LEAH: Yeah, the 'arnica' must have helped

Beat.

TOM: Last night, I didn't force you did I?

LEAH: *(shakes her head)* No. Tom, I stayed 'cos I wanted to

TOM: How do you feel?

LEAH: Hungry

TOM: In that case, brunch – what will it be? Toast, cereal – we've got coco pops, bacon sandwiches?

LEAH: Whatever you're having

TOM: I say you can't beat a bacon sarnie first thing, I've got some on the go already

Leah smiles. He exits to the kitchen. Leah sits down, pulls the book over to her, smiles.

TOM: *(from off)* Tea or coffee?

LEAH: Coffee, milky, three sugars

Her phone buzzes in the pocket of the dressing gown. She takes it out and reads the message. Her face falls. Tom enters.

TOM: Good God Leah

Startled she looks up and shoves the phone into her pocket.

Three sugars? You'll give yourself diabetes

She laughs.

LEAH: Only in the first cup of the day, to help with the shock of having to get up

He laughs.

TOM: She used to have hot chocolate I should have offered that we've still got some in in the cupboard

LEAH: Coffee's fine, perfect

He nods.

TOM: I used to make it for her every morning before school whilst her mother lectured her about why she shouldn't be having it. Every morning

He exits to the kitchen.

LEAH: *(referring to the book)* To Kill A Mockingbird, "You never really understand a person until you consider things from his point of view... until you climb into his skin and walk around in it."

TOM: You've read it?

LEAH: No, it was on the back. I like the sound of it though

TOM: You'd enjoy it. Once I've finished you can have a read... if you like

LEAH: Yeah. *(quickly)* I'm not thick you know

TOM: I never thought you were

LEAH: I don't know what you think of me. What you think I am

TOM: I don't think anything Leah

LEAH: Even if I go back?

TOM: What?

LEAH: I can't stay here forever

The smell of bacon burning and the sound of the smoke alarm going off.

(jumping up) Shit, shit, shit

He runs to the kitchen and starts jumping, cursing and waving a tea towel over the alarm.

TOM: Bloody thing, urrgghh, shit, stop you bastard

Leah begins to giggle, he catches her and can't resist a smile.

Funny is it?

She laughs and nods, he joins in. The alarm stops.

    I'm afraid the bacon's off the menu

LEAH: Coco pops?

TOM: Coco pops it is... Gill used to say I was a hypocrite... no sugar in my coffee but a huge bowl of coco pops

LEAH: You miss her

Tom nods, picks up the ketchup and makes to leave

    The picture in the bedroom, the three of you, how old is Sophie?

TOM: Seven. Her godmother's wedding.

    She was a bridesmaid but kept getting me to pretend she was the bride and walk behind her holding her dress *(he laughs at the memory)*. Me and her Mum were amazed, she usually refused to wear dresses and she'd told her poor nanna that if ever she got married she'd be doing it in trousers!

Leah laughs.

    I'd never lay a finger on her

LEAH: I know

TOM: So why doesn't Gill? I've known you five minutes, I've known her twenty years

SCENE 11

Café. Gill sits. She pours tea from a pot. Tom has just arrived and is taking off his coat.

TOM: You're here. Sorry, I'm not late am I? *(glancing at his watch)* It was 9.30 / we said?

GILL: I was early. Couldn't sleep

TOM: Right. Sorry to hear / that

GILL: I ordered you a tea. I didn't mean to, it just came / out

TOM: That's fine. Great. Just what I need

Pause. Tom sits.

So…? *(beat)* How are you feeling?

Gill scoffs, shakes her head.

GILL: Is this what it's come to?

TOM: What?

GILL: You sound like my fucking counsellor

TOM: What do you want me to say?

GILL: She's living with you

TOM: -

GILL: Did you think I didn't know?

TOM: No / I

GILL: Everyone on the street knows, you know the way people do when it's something private. (*beat*) Do you know what it looks like?

TOM: She's in trouble

GILL: Is she? Makes two of you then. Everyone knows your suspended; the kids, the parents, the teachers, you should hear the rumours

TOM: I'm sorry if it's difficult for you to be there

GILL: I'm not. I'm signed off. Sue keeps me posted though – apparently it's all over Snapchat and I've seen the Facebook page… covered in abuse

TOM: I know

GILL: Did she move in that night? Sophie's birthday?

TOM: There's / nothing going on

GILL: And you see I was thinking where, where does she sleep? It's either in my daughter's bed my missing daughter's bed which is truly, truly fucked up or, and I'm not sure if this is better or worse, with you, in our bed and either way / I feel

TOM: She sleeps in our bed

Gill sobs.

On her own, on her own Gill

Gill laughs.

GILL: Right, right

TOM: It's true

GILL: And is that before or after you've had sex with her?

TOM: Oh for Christ's sake

GILL: Come on Tom

TOM: What?

GILL: Stop lying to me.

TOM: I'm not

GILL: I'm not stupid

TOM: I know that

GILL: Well come on then. You have, haven't you? It's on a fucking plate

TOM: No

GILL: You must have tucked her in, rubbed cream on her bruises, comforted her?

TOM: *(quietly)* Yes but not like that

GILL: Hugged her, kissed her on the forehead, stroked her face as she fell asleep... and where have you drawn the line?

TOM: Stop it

GILL: And where do you sleep? Hm? On the sofa?

Beat.

TOM: I sleep in Sophie's bed

Beat.

GILL: Sophie's bed?

He nods.

Have you washed her sheets?

He shakes his head.

TOM: I didn't want Leah to be in there

GILL: *(hearing her name for the first time)* Leah

TOM: I have to help her. Doesn't the Church preach 'love thy neighbour'?

GILL: You bastard

TOM: I'm sorry.

GILL: You fucking bastard

TOM: He hits her, makes her do / things

GILL: Do you see how it looks? You're suspended from school for inappropriate conduct and you're living with a girl who looks like your daughter.

TOM: She's older – in her twenties

GILL: Were you having an affair? Before Sophie left even? Did you do things with her to stop yourself doing things to Sophie? Because Sophie didn't like it?

TOM: Gill please, people are looking

GILL: Where did you even meet her? Where do you meet a girl like that? At the fucking dentist? We've been together for twenty years. Do me the decency of telling me the truth

TOM: *(slowly)* I hired her

GILL: -

TOM: She was an escort and I hired her

GILL: -

TOM: She dressed up as a school girl for me

GILL: -

TOM: Because I missed Sophie

GILL: -

TOM: It was never sexual

Gill is still. Pause.

Gill?

GILL: And you expect me to believe you're not sleeping with her? That you didn't touch that girl

TOM: Gill I am telling you the truth. I'm helping her

GILL: -

TOM: She needs me

GILL: Needs you?

TOM: She / is

GILL: She needs you?

TOM: Yes

GILL: And what about what I need?

Pause.

> It's been seven months, two weeks and / three days

TOM: Three days I know

Beat.

GILL: Is she dead?

They look at each other.

> They've stopped looking. *(beat)* People keep telling me life is precious but... is it? I wake up every morning and I just feel grey. I sit in my room, my mother goes out, and nothing in the house moves. The light just changes outside. But God says life is a gift so I keep trying. Oh sod it.

She brushes him away and leaves.

> Do what you want

SCENE 12

London. A park. Mark waits. Leah enters.

LEAH: You wanted to see me

MARK: Yeah, thank you for coming, I wasn't / sure you would

LEAH: I'm not coming back

Mark nods.

MARK: You look good. Wherever you are, whatever you're doing it's / working

LEAH: I haven't got long / so

MARK: I'm sorry

LEAH: Right

MARK: I mean it Lea, I lost it

LEAH: Yeah, you did

MARK: I'm so sorry. Seriously. *(moves to touch her face)* Look at your little face

LEAH: Don't

MARK: I thought I'd lost you

LEAH: You have lost me…

MARK: I'm sorry alright, you just made me so upset

LEAH: -

MARK: You lied about meeting him. You lied to me Leah

LEAH: I'm sorry

MARK: I just couldn't cope with the lies, that's all it was. Do you understand?

LEAH: -

MARK: I was out of control, I hate this, I hate being like this. I'm sorry alright

LEAH: I have to go

She starts to leave.

MARK: Please Leah... Leah... I know where you are

Leah stops, turns

LEAH: What?

MARK: I know where you're living

LEAH: How?

MARK: I put a tracking app on your phone

LEAH: You did what?

MARK: So you were safe. When you went on jobs

LEAH: -

MARK: Don't look at me like that, I did it for you

LEAH: No, you're lying

MARK: Twenty-three Westgarth Gardens

LEAH: *(she's shocked)* Then why haven't you / come to find me?

MARK: So you're living with him, the guy from the park?

LEAH: I don't have to explain

She starts to leave.

MARK: Leah, he's using you. He's using you. Can't you see that?

LEAH: You've got no idea

MARK: What if his daughter comes back? What will happen to you then? He needs you now but... Lea please, please don't give up on us

LEAH: Why? Why shouldn't I?

MARK: Because it's us, we've been through such a lot and I love you and I just need you to give me one more chance

Beat.

Look, I know I've fucked things up but I can't lose you. I'll be better now. Like I used to be. You used to call me your angel, do you remember that? Said I gave the best hugs you'd ever had. You said I was the first person, since your Dad left, that had ever really understood you, do you remember saying that?

Leah nods

And on that very first night we met, you told me you thought no-one would ever want you, and then I kissed you and you were so surprised you started to cry. (*He begins to stroke her arms and slowly takes her hands*) And then we went back to mine and I promised I'd never leave you and I won't. We can get through anything you and me, Lea. Will you come home?

She looks at him, touches his face, shakes her head 'no' and leaves.

Please don't stop loving me

He is left alone.

SCENE 13

Leah sits in the lounge at the coffee table applying last touches of make-up whilst watching 'A Streetcar Named Desire'. Her phone pings. She smiles a small smile and replies. Front door slams.

LEAH: Ah, you're back! *(jumping up and facing the door she knows Tom is about to come through)* Does this say waitress to you?

Tom enters slowly, he is covered in egg and has grazes on his face.

Oh my God. Tom, what happened?

TOM: They were waiting for me when I came out of Tesco's

LEAH: Who?

TOM: Kids. Teenagers

LEAH: *(gently taking off his coat)* Let's get this off. *(he complies)* That's better. Do you want to get in the shower, or I could run you a bath?

TOM: First egg right on top of my head. Perfect shot. I thought I'd been shat on. *(beat)* Would have been a bloody big bird

He laughs, Leah smiles weakly.

I dropped all my bags. I'd spent over fifteen pounds so I could use that voucher

LEAH: Did no-one help?

TOM: I think someone was trying to scoop up my things but I was running to the car. Praying I wouldn't trip or have a bloody heart attack

LEAH: You're bleeding?

TOM: I think they ran out of eggs

LEAH: Stones?

TOM: *(nods)* When I got to the car they'd slashed the tyres... People were watching, laughing, one girl was filming it on her phone. And they were shouting. Shouting awful things. I recognised one of the voices. *(beat)* Laura Tyler. She used to like me

LEAH: Couldn't you see their faces?

TOM: They were covered. I didn't know what to do so I got in my car and closed my eyes. They were rocking it, banging on the windows. I think I was crying. Silly old fool *(he tries to smile)*

Leah takes his hand.

TOM: Someone must have told a manager because she came out and said she was calling the police, that she had them on CCTV. *(beat)* I sat there until the police came. They took me inside, gave me a cup of tea, asked me some questions. *(beat)* But they were... I could see in their faces what they were thinking... No smoke without fire

LEAH: You've done nothing wrong

TOM: Will it be like this forever?

LEAH: No. Maybe I should leave?

TOM: No, no. That wouldn't help. You're the only one who believes me

LEAH: Things will get better. Look, why don't you have a shower and I'll make us some food. We'll have a 'girl's night in'. I recorded 'Breakfast at Tiffany's' for us

He smiles and properly looks at her.

TOM: Shit, what about your interview?

LEAH: It doesn't matter

TOM: Yes it does. Go!

LEAH: Tom, I'm not leaving you, not after...

TOM: Leah please don't let me spoil this for you

LEAH: I'll be able to go tomorrow and if not... I'll find somewhere else

TOM: But

LEAH: Look, no. Shower

TOM: You're very sweet

He exits for the shower. Leah watches him go.

SCENE 14

Lights come up on Tom and Leah. It is the morning after Scene 13. Tom sits on the sofa and Leah lays with her head in his lap, his hand on her hair. The television is on low in the background and empty plates are on the floor. They both wear their nightclothes. Doorbell rings. They start and wake up. Tom exits to answer the door.

TOM: *(from off)* Gill?

GILL: Can I come in?

TOM: Er, yes

Tom re-enters with Gill. She surveys the scene.

GILL: Oh for God's / sake

TOM: Gill

GILL: I… / I

TOM: We fell asleep / watching

GILL: None of my business. I'll come back later

TOM: Gill stay, have a coffee, please

He exits to put the kettle on.

GILL: *(to Leah)* I know you're suffering but you are destroying him

Gill puts her hand in her coat pocket and brings out a number on a piece of paper, she hands it to Leah.

Women's Refuge. That's what you need. Not him

Tom re-enters.

TOM: It'll just be a couple of minutes

Suddenly Leah leaps off the sofa and exits, we hear her vomit off stage. Gill watches her. Beat.

GILL: I heard what happened yesterday

TOM: No less than I deserve

GILL: There's more abuse on the Facebook page, messages pouring in

TOM: Just come round to gloat have you?

GILL: *(hurt)* Is that what you think of me?

TOM: -

GILL: I was worried about you

Leah re-enters and sits on the couch.

TOM: You OK?

GILL: Too much to drink?

Leah shakes her head and doesn't make eye contact. Awkward pause.

TOM: Right, coffee?

Doorbell rings.

    I'll just

Tom exits to answer door.

GILL: *(to Leah)* Every morning?

Leah nods.

How long?

LEAH: Week or so

TOM: *(to Leah, from off)* They're for you

As Tom returns and gives Leah the tube Gill walks past him.

Gill?

He follows. Leah undoes the flowers and reads the note that accompanies them. She smiles.

Gill?

Tom returns.

What happened?

LEAH: Nothing

TOM: Leah

LEAH: I don't know. She just went

Leah's phone buzzes. He watches her read the text.

TOM: *(as Leah puts down the phone)* You know what he's trying to do

LEAH: I know Tom, I'll be / careful

TOM: Careful? *(suddenly realising)* That means he knows you're here?

LEAH: He found out

TOM: Did you tell him?

LEAH: No, of course not

TOM: Then how did he find out? Leah?

LEAH: He put a tracker on my phone

TOM: A tracker?

LEAH: It was on there from before, it sounds worse than it is

Tom's phone rings, he looks to see who is calling.

TOM: Shit

LEAH: What?

He answers phone.

TOM: Steve… What's happened? …Right… Where? I want to be there… I have to tell Gill, I'll call you back

Tom hangs up. Leah looks at him.

They've found remains

LEAH: Sophie?

TOM: They're not sure. A member of the public's put it on bloody Facebook

LEAH: Oh / Tom *(she goes to him)*

TOM: I need to be there. I'll collect Gill on the way

Tom leaves. Leah sits on the sofa. Breathes. Takes out a pregnancy test from her bag, looks at it. Mark appears. Leah looks up and sees him. She screams and stuffs the test back into her bag

MARK: Back door was open, thought I'd surprise you

LEAH: Fuck s / ake

MARK: Looks like it worked. *(he laughs)* Is that his dressing gown?

LEAH: Yeah, I borrowed / it

MARK: Suits you. *(beat)* You got the flowers then?

LEAH: Yeah, they're beau / tiful

MARK: Wages from my first pay packet

LEAH: You got a job?

MARK: Yeah

LEAH: Doing what?

MARK: Working on cars

LEAH: That's brilliant

MARK: Thought it was about time I sorted myself out. *(looking around)* This is lovely, isn't I? Very nice. *(indicating the picture of Sophie on the wall)* Is that her?

LEAH: Yeah

Mark looks from the picture to Leah to the picture.

Yes

MARK: No wonder / he

LEAH: Yeah, yeah

MARK: Any news?

LEAH: What do you care?

MARK: *(hurt)* -

LEAH: They've found remains but they're not sure

MARK: Shit.

Beat.

>Have you missed me?

Leah rushes to be sick again. Mark looks to see what she hid in her bag. Pulls out the pregnancy test. Moments pass. He puts it back. Leah re-enters. They look at each other.

>Was that your answer?

LEAH: Sorry

MARK: Hangover?

LEAH: *(she shakes her head)* No, just a bug

Leah sits on the sofa. Mark fishes in his pocket and pulls out a curlywurly

MARK: Curlywurly to take the taste away?

She laughs, shakes her head.

>Come on, you know you want it, you love your curlywurly – woo woo. *(he mimes it as his penis)* Go

on, just a little bite, it'll help with the taste. *(he simulates it being an aeroplane flying toward her mouth)* Neeeoow, into the tunnel. Go on

He puts it to her lips and she takes a small bite

Good girl. *(beat)* Do you wanna come home Lea?

LEAH: Maybe

He nods.

MARK: I meant what I said, the other day in the park

She looks at him.

MARK: I'm sorry. *(beat)* We could go slow. Date for a while. I can treat you now I've got a job. As many curlywurly's as you like

She laughs. Beat.

I'm not all bad, am I?

LEAH: *(gently)* I know

MARK: *(pulling her to him so that she rests on his chest)* I'll look after you this time. No more escorting. No more secrets. Just us

Beat.

If you feel better later you could come round? I'll cook

LEAH: You?

MARK: Yeah, why not?

LEAH: Can I let you know?

MARK: Course

LEAH: You better go

MARK: Yeah, right. Call me, yeah?

LEAH: *(flirting)* Maybe

Mark smiles and exits.

SCENE 15

Lounge. Leah is asleep on the sofa, still wearing the dressing-gown. The door opens, Gill and Tom enter. They are both exhausted. Gill walks past Leah to go upstairs

LEAH: Any news?

TOM: Not yet. They said to expect a call sometime this evening *(beat. He looks after Gill)* She wanted to be in Sophie's room

LEAH: Do you want some tea?

TOM: God no, I'm swimming in it

He closes his eyes. Leah watches him.

    This could be it

He exhales deeply.

LEAH: Did you go, to the site?

Tom nods.

TOM: Couldn't get anywhere near

LEAH: So where did you go?

TOM: The station. She's inconsolable

He looks at Leah.

    We've been sat in an airless room all afternoon drinking tepid fucking tea. Then she suddenly decided she needed to be –

Tom's phone buzzes. He looks at it.

>Steve. *(beat)* I'm not ready

He watches it ringing.

LEAH: Tom

TOM: It's better not knowing than

The phone stops.

>Shit

They look at each other. Moments pass. It rings again. He picks up.

>Hello... *(he breathes hard trying to get hold of himself)* ...Yes, yes, thank you, thank you... yes, I understand, thank you... You too

During the last part of the phone call Gill has appeared in the doorway holding Matilda – the toy rabbit. She stands very still. Gill and Leah look at Tom.

>It wasn't her

GILL: Ohhhh, Thank you, thank you God, thank you God, thank you God, thank you God

Gill cries until the cry turns into a guttural scream and she falls to her knees. Tom goes to her. They cling to each other

>I thought it was her. I thought it I thought *(She sobs. Her crying is out of control, violent and raw)*

TOM: *(looking at Leah)* They were fox bones

Leah watches for a moment then leaves to go upstairs taking the pregnancy test with her. After some time Gill recovers. She can no longer make eye contact with Tom.

GILL: I should go

TOM: You don't have to

GILL: Yes I do. It's humiliating

She gets up and wipes her face.

       You shouldn't have seen that

TOM: You're my wife

GILL: Am I? *(beat)* Can I take this? *(she holds up Matilda)*

TOM: I'd rather... yes, yes, of course

Leah enters. She has changed into her clothes and put on some make-up, she has a bag over her shoulder.

LEAH: Sorry, you need some space, I'm just going to pop out

TOM: It's fine

LEAH: I have to go out anyway

TOM: Where to?

LEAH: Interview in town

TOM: Where?

LEAH: A restaurant

TOM: Which one?

LEAH: Tom?

TOM: I'm interested

GILL: Fuck sake

She makes to leave.

TOM: Gill wait

GILL: I'm not standing here while you have a lover's tiff

TOM: I'm worried about her

LEAH: Tom, I'm fine. I'll see you later *(she leaves)*

TOM: I'm not doing anything/ with

GILL: You know she's pregnant, don't you?

TOM: -

GILL: Congratulations

TOM: What? I

GILL: You didn't know?

TOM: Pregnant?

GILL: This is what can happen when you have / sex

TOM: It's not mine

GILL: Really?

TOM: We've never had / sex

GILL: It can happen the first time

TOM: Jesus Christ Gill, you have to believe me

GILL: Do I?

TOM: -

GILL: I haven't got the energy to fight for you. I thought my girl was in the ground today but she's not so I'm gonna go home and have a fuck off glass of wine and go to bed

TOM: It must be his. Don't you see? Fuck. Fuck it

He scrabbles to find his phone.

GILL: This is… *(tailing off)* madness

Gill starts to leave.

TOM: *(whilst texting)* For God's sake, it's not mine

GILL: It's fine Tom. You have my blessing

She leaves.

TOM: IT'S NOT MINE

SCENE 16

Classical music plays. Leah is in the doorway. Mark looks at her She smiles, so does he. He signals for her to twirl, she does so confidently.

LEAH: I let myself in

MARK: Touché

She smiles

> Wow, you look... fit

Leah spins

> Would madam like a seat?

As she walks past him he slaps her bottom

LEAH: *(in mock horror)* Oi, this is a first date, remember. Behave yourself

She smiles.

> What we having?

MARK: Pasta

LEAH: *(teasing)* Ooo, adventurous

MARK: I'm trying Lea

LEAH: I can see that. I appreciate it

Pause.

MARK: So, any news... Sophie?

LEAH: It wasn't her

MARK: You're still his surrogate then?

Leah looks at him.

> Sorry, sorry. (*beat*) So what you going to have to drink, I've got vodka, beer, wine?

LEAH: Could I just have water?

MARK: Water? That's not like you Leah

LEAH: My tummy's still a bit delicate

MARK: Course. yeah, yeah, water, right. Coming right up

He leaves. She looks around.

LEAH: *(calling to the kitchen)* I like the music

MARK: Yeah?

LEAH: Yeah

MARK: Classical mix... found it on Youtube. Didn't cost me a fucking penny

He gives Leah the water and they sit opposite.

> *(raising his glass)* There you go. To us. A fresh start

LEAH: I'd like that

She smiles, they chink glasses. Beat.

MARK: *(smiling)* Lied again

LEAH: Sorry?

MARK: Earlier

LEAH: About what?

MARK: Hmmm, what could I mean? *(he stands)* Let's have a think shall we

LEAH: Mark, you're scaring me

MARK: Am I? Do you think that's unfair?

LEAH: What?

MARK: 'Cos I think it's unfair that you make me feel like this

LEAH: Like what?

MARK: Like I'm always in the wrong, like it's always me that's doing stuff to you when / really

LEAH: I don't / understand

MARK: No-one sees that it's you, the way you string me along

LEAH: I / don't

MARK: Make me look like a twat

LEAH: Please calm / down

MARK: Does he know you're here?

LEAH: Who

MARK: COME ON LEAH

LEAH: No

Mark laughs.

MARK: Did you lie to him too? Tom? *(smirks)* No rescue party then. You see this is what happens, when you start telling lies

LEAH: *(standing, approaching him)* Mark, I was just staying there, there was nothing in it

MARK: Really?

LEAH: Yes

MARK: Sure about that?

LEAH: Yes

MARK: Sure there's nothing you need to tell me?

LEAH: -

MARK: Hm? Can't hear?

LEAH: There's nothing

MARK: Wrong answer. *(he grabs her arms and lefts them to the side, level with her shoulders)* One chance to put it right... go

LEAH: Mark, I don't know what you want me to say

In a quick movement he raises his arm as if to punch her in the stomach. She recoils covering her belly.

MARK: What's the matter Leah? Is there something precious in there?

LEAH: How did you know?

MARK: So there is? A little souvenir from your stay?

LEAH: No, no Mark it's yours

MARK: Yeah, you would say that, wouldn't you

LEAH: It is

MARK: Don't lie to me again Leah

LEAH: For fuck's sake Mark it's not his

MARK: Don't you 'fuck's sake' me... I caught you together, remember? Chips in the park

LEAH: Yeah, *chips*

MARK: Couldn't wait to move in could you, soon as he offered

LEAH: I slept / by myself

MARK: Shagging him in his wife's bed or his daughters? Both fucked up really. Or did that intensify the orgasm?

LEAH: We've nev / er

MARK: You were wearing his dressing gown

LEAH: Mark

MARK: Do you like it? Do you like it with him? Big, powerful man. Is he grateful? Does he cry? Does he call you Sophie? Or is it because you miss your step-dad? Is that it? Yeah, it's 'cos you miss your step-dad

LEAH: No

MARK: You can't keep it Leah

LEAH: What do you mean?

MARK: It would tear us apart

LEAH: I am keeping it

He shakes his head.

MARK: You've got to do something for me now. To make up for all the lies

LEAH: What?

MARK: It's easy. It won't hurt *(he produces two pills)*

LEAH: No

MARK: It'll just die

LEAH: No Mark

MARK: Bit of bleeding and it's gone

LEAH: It's *your* baby

MARK: It's perfectly safe, they give it to you in hospital. Just two little tablets, come on Leah, come on

LEAH: *(desperate)* Please Mark

He moves to her and grabs her by the throat, leads her to the table and forces her to lay on the table. He straddles her. Throughout Leah struggles. He tries to open her mouth but she won't allow him to. Eventually she lashes out and hurts him. Still managing to hold her, he reaches beneath the sofa and pulls out a knitting needle.

MARK: It's your choice

Leah screams

LEAH: *(slowly)* Okay, okay

MARK: Good girl, open wide. Here's one. good girl. Here comes the other

Mark sits her up and helps Leah to drink the water to wash down the tablets.

Good girl, good girl

In a sudden movement, Leah spits the water and tablets in his face and kicks him hard in the groin. He doubles in pain and she runs. Classical music continues to play.

SCENE 17

London. Tom's house. Lounge. Leah is in the same clothes as the previous scene. She is in a state. She throws on her parker then opens her rucksack and begins shoving in the remaining items of hers that she has gathered to take. Tom enters.

TOM: Oh Leah, thank God

LEAH: Shit

TOM: I've been going out of my mind

LEAH: I lied

TOM: I know. I guessed

LEAH: I'm sorry

TOM: It doesn't matter

LEAH: Yes it does

TOM: It doesn't. *(registering the coat and rucksack)* Where are you going?

LEAH: Away

TOM: Why?

LEAH: He's lost it

TOM: Did he hurt you again?

She nods.

Did he hurt the baby?

Beat. She looks at him.

LEAH: -

TOM: Gill told me

LEAH: I would've told/ you

TOM: I know

LEAH: I thought he wanted me

TOM: Oh Leah. *(beat)* We'll call the police, tell them what happened

LEAH: It'll be my word against his

TOM: They'll believe you, trust me

LEAH: No

TOM: He'll be arrested

LEAH: I SAID NO

TOM: Leah, I am begging you, please, please, please stay… I need you

LEAH: Don't. Please don't say that. I can't, I… can't. Tom. It's not just me now… if anything happened… I would never forgive myself. So I have to go. I called a helpline, they've given me a place in a refuge

TOM: Where?

LEAH: Manchester

TOM: Manchester?!

LEAH: I'm lucky to get anywhere

TOM: Well, where in Manchester?

LEAH: They told me not to say

TOM: What about money?

LEAH: I've got a little bit... from before

TOM: Let me. *(he finds his wallet and gives her sixty pounds)* For when you're there

LEAH: No, I can't take your money

TOM: You can buy the first portion of chips when I come and visit

She smiles.

Call me when you get there

LEAH: I can't, the tracker on my phone – I threw it in the river

TOM: Use someone else's. *(he gives her the label from his wallet)* Here. Don't lose it

She hugs him and begins to leave.

No, no I can't let you go on your own

LEAH: Tom

TOM: I'm taking you

LEAH: To Manchester?

TOM: If that's where you need to go

LEAH: I can't ask you / to

TOM: You're not asking, I'm insisting

Beat. She looks at him.

LEAH: I'm so sorry

TOM: You have absolutely nothing to be sorry for

She hoists the rucksack on to her back.

TOM: Let's go

They exit.

SCENE 18

London. The bridge. Tom stands alone. Gill enters.

GILL: Thought I might find you here. (*Tom turns*). Are you OK? Stupid question. How are you feeling?

TOM: Now who's the councillor?

GILL: Sorry

He smiles at her.

Have you heard from her?

TOM: A text, yesterday, "I'm fine. Don't worry"

GILL: It's only been three days

TOM: I wanted to save her

GILL: You did

Beat.

TOM: You thought I was sleeping with her

GILL: I

TOM: Other people thought so too so you're not alone. *(beat)* I just wanted to look after her. That was all. Nothing more. Nothing seedy. It wasn't like that. It was pure. Oh fuck it. It sounds like bullshit when I say it out loud

They sit for a few moments in silence.

GILL: I came to tell you something

TOM: *(quickly)* Sophie?

GILL: *(shakes her head)* Emily withdrew her allegation this morning

TOM: *(stunned)* What?

GILL: Said you didn't touch her inappropriately...

TOM: She

GILL: Said you were just being kind

TOM: -

GILL: Sue rang me this morning, it's not official yet. Emily's parents were mortified

Tom looks at her

> After what happened the other day... outside the supermarket, Emily fell to pieces and it all came out

Beat. She breaks. Tom stares out. Gill starts to leave. He looks at her.

GILL: I'm so sorry

He looks out. Gill exits. Tom climbs on to the edge of the bridge.

> *(rushing to him)* No, please. Please

TOM: It's fine. I'm just dangling my legs

GILL: What?

TOM: Dangling my legs. It feels nice

GILL: Oh God

TOM: *(gently)* Why don't you join me?

GILL: I thought / you

TOM: I'd love nothing more

GILL: What?

TOM: I'd love to jump. To know it was finally over. It only takes two to three minutes

GILL: For fuck sake

TOM: Your brain is flooded with endorphins. Like you've just taken a bag of E

GILL: Stop it

TOM: What?

GILL: -

TOM: I wouldn't. I can't

GILL: No

TOM: Not fear. I'm way past that

Beat.

> Sophie could come back

Gill sighs. Tom ignores her.

> Any day. It happens. It can be years and years / and then

GILL: And if they find her body?

TOM: *(takes a deep breath)* Until that day comes. So you don't have to worry

GILL: But I do worry

He looks at her.

>Can I come home?

Tom doesn't answer, which is an answer in itself. Gill nods. They look out.

SCENE 19

The beach, on the rocks. Leah waits. She is seven months pregnant. Moments pass. Tom enters.

TOM: Leah

LEAH: You're late

They smile at each other.

TOM: Look at you

LEAH: *(laughing)* I know, I've ballooned!

TOM: It suits you

She laughs.

      How is she?

LEAH: Energetic

TOM: *(indicates the bump)* Getting ready

LEAH: Yeah. Only two months to go

TOM: I've missed you

They hug.

      Shall we sit?

LEAH: God yeah, my ankles are like tree trunks

They sit.

TOM: So, how is everything, how's the flat?

LEAH: Not bad, one bedroom, a stain in the bath and view of the carpark but I just close my eyes and focus on the seagulls

Tom smiles.

It's lovely. Peaceful

TOM: Better than Manchester?

LEAH: God yeah. And Portsoy's only a bus ride away. I've always wanted to live abroad!

He laughs.

He'll never find me here. He's never been out of London, Scotland wouldn't cross his mind

TOM: And he's still not tried to contact you?

LEAH: Tom, stop worrying

He smiles.

TOM: Sorry

She smiles.

LEAH: What about you? How are things?

TOM: There's not been a lead in months. I think the police think she's dead or doesn't want to be found. *(beat)* but they've not recovered a body and she wouldn't do this to us so I... I keep going. I put things on the Facebook page, Twitter, Instagram. I found a computer programme that uses bone structure to work out how someone will look as they get older. I generated her image. It's terrifying. I use that picture now, instead of the old one. Occasionally someone calls but... And once in a while I just get in my car and drive; places she liked to go. I even went to Scarborough for a weekend – her favourite childhood holiday. I never stop. Will never stop unless...

Beat

LEAH: And Gill?

TOM: Moved back in last month. We're taking it slow. Rebuilding

LEAH: How is she?

TOM: She talks to God a lot. That seems to help

LEAH: And what helps you?

TOM: Reading. Slipping in and out of other people's lives

She smiles.

LEAH: Do you talk to Gill – about Sophie?

TOM: We mark the occasions but we don't dwell. Not together anyway. *(beat)* Gill says we mustn't let our tragedy define us. I say we have no choice. *(he smirks)* So we don't talk about it

Leah smiles. They sit for a few moments in silence.

LEAH: I wish I had someone to do this *(indicates the baby)* with me, tell me if I'm getting it wrong

TOM: You'll get it wrong all the time

LEAH: What?

TOM: Everyone does

LEAH: I'm scared

TOM: I'll come and help

LEAH: Really? Really, you'd do that?

TOM: I'd love it. Maybe one day I could bring Gill?

LEAH: I'd like that

TOM: She's good with babies, no nonsense

LEAH: What about you?

TOM: Oh, I'm gooey

LEAH: Gooey?

TOM: Soppy, soft... a push-over

LEAH: *(she laughs)* Good team then?

TOM: Yeah, we were

Beat.

LEAH: Do you think she'll be like Mark?

TOM: She'll be the way you bring her up

LEAH: He'll be in her genes

TOM: But you're her Mum

Beat.

LEAH: *(suddenly, reaching into her bag)* Ooo, nearly forgot... I finished the book

TOM: What did you think?

LEAH: It made me want to scream

He laughs.

TOM: You'd love the film... Gregory Peck as Atticus Finch

LEAH: Oh wow

Beat.

> And *(she reaches into her pocket and takes out his handkerchief from Scene 4)*

TOM: *(smiling)* My handkerchief... no you keep it

LEAH: No, it's got your initials on it

He takes it. Beat.

TOM: Did you think you'd find him...your Dad?

She looks at him.

LEAH: Yes. No. I dunno. Is that stupid?

Tom shakes his head.

> I just thought maybe... that he might still be here. That I'll bump into him coming out of Poundland or Tesco or... that I'll be walking around the town and I'll see him, sunglasses on top of his head, wearing some ancient rock band t-shirt and eating jelly babies

Tom smiles.

When I first got here I'd go to Portsoy and sit by the war memorial every Saturday afternoon. I remember him saying there was no better place to enjoy an ice-cream so... just in case

TOM: Yeah

LEAH: Truth is, he probably wouldn't even recognise me

Moments pass.

TOM: Shall we get some chips?

LEAH: Yeah. *(beat)* How long do you keep hoping? Keep hoping for someone to come back?

TOM: Until they do

Leah nods

They look out.

Lights fade.

THE END